TOYS AND GAMES
THEN AND NOW

by Robin Nelson

first step nonfiction

Lerner Publications Company · Minneapolis

Toys and games are fun.

Toys and games have
changed over time.

Long ago, children played
with homemade dolls.

Now, children play with dolls that come from stores.

Long ago, children built with big wooden blocks.

Now, children build with little
plastic blocks.

Long ago, children rode rocking horses.

Now, children ride bicycles.

ST. PAUL DAILY
NEWS PHOTO

Long ago, children played
with **marbles** at **recess**.

Now, children play in colorful playgrounds at recess.

Long ago, children moved
toy trains with their hands.

Now, toy trains can move by themselves.

Long ago, children played
jacks.

Now, children play video games.

Long ago, children played
with teddy bears.

Now, children **snuggle** with
all kinds of stuffed animals.

Toys and Games in the United States

1610
First rocking
horse made.

1839
First bicycle
with pedals
invented.

1816
First bicycle
that could
be steered.

1901
Joshua Lionel
Cohen sells the
first electric train.

1903
First teddy
bear appears
in stores.

1959
First Barbie
doll sold.

1949
Legos®
invented.

1972
First video
game invented.

Toys and Games Facts

 The first toys we know of were made over 2,000 years ago. Children in ancient Egypt played with balls, tops, and dolls.

 When Legos® were first invented, they came in only two colors—red and white.

 Teddy bears are named after President Theodore "Teddy" Roosevelt. President Roosevelt liked to go bear hunting, but once he saved a bear cub.

The Lionel train company makes more than one million electric train cars a year.

 Long ago, marbles were made of stone, pottery, clay, or china. Now, most marbles are made of glass.

 Long ago, dolls were made out of things that people had around the house. Some were made of corn husks or dried apples.

Glossary

jacks – a game played by picking up metal pieces while a ball bounces

marbles – small glass balls

 plastic – a material things are made of

recess – a time for play during the school day

 snuggle – to hold close

Index

The photographs in this book were reproduced through the courtesy of: Colorado Historical Society, Garrison Collection (#CHS.X6115), front cover; Digital Vision, p. 2; © Minnesota Historical Society/CORBIS, pp. 3, 14, 22 (top); McCord Museum of Canadian History, Montreal, p. 4; © Todd Strand/Independent Picture Service, pp. 5, 7, 15, 22 (middle); Minnesota Historical Society, p. 6; Photo by Albert Munson, Minnesota Historical Society, p. 8; © Diane Meyer, p. 9; Photo by St. Paul Daily News, Minnesota Historical Society, pp. 10, 22 (second from top, second from bottom); PhotoDisc, p. 11; © Taxi/Getty Images, p. 12; © Roger Ressmeyer/CORBIS, p. 13; © The Art Archive, p, 16; © Debbie Turnrose, pp. 17, 22 (bottom).

Lerner Publications Company
A division of Lerner Publishing Group, Inc.
241 First Avenue North
Minneapolis, MN 55401 U.S.A.

Website address: www.lernerbooks.com

Library of Congress Cataloging-in-Publication Data

Nelson, Robin, 1971–
    Toys and games then and now / by Robin Nelson.
      p. cm. — (First step nonfiction)
    Summary: Briefly describes how toys and games have changed through the years, including such topics as how playgrounds differ and how today's toys relate to those of the past.
    Includes index.
    ISBN-13: 978–0–8225–4644–3 (lib. bdg. : alk. paper)
    ISBN-10: 0–8225–4644–2 (lib. bdg. : alk. paper)
    1. Toys—United States—History—Juvenile literature. 2. Games—United States—History—Juvenile literature. [1. Toys—History. 2. Games—History.] I. Title. II. Series.
    GV1218.5 .N45 2003
    790.1'33—dc21
                                                                      2002010679

Manufactured in the United States of America
5 6 7 8 9 10 – DP – 13 12 11 10 09 08